THE
BEST
OF
SUCCESS

Compiled by
Wynn Davis

Within the pages of this handbook,
are the prominent ideas that can serve
as the keystones for building
a successful life.

This collection is filled with quotations
that motivate and inspire us to reach for
life's most fulfilling achievements.

The power to be the best is within all of
us. As we get close to these ideas, and
work with this power, the best of
success will truly be ours.

TABLE OF CONTENTS

BELIEF

Belief is the knowledge that we can do something. It's the inner feeling that what we undertake, we can accomplish. For the most part, all of us have the ability to look at something and know whether or not we can do it. So, in belief there is power: our eyes are opened; our opportunities become plain; our visions become realities.

He can who thinks he can, and he can't who thinks he can't. This is an inexorable, indisputable law.

ORISON SWETT MARDEN

What the mind of man can conceive and believe, the mind of man can achieve.

NAPOLEON HILL

The only thing that stands between a man and what he wants from life is often merely the will to try it and the faith to believe that it is possible.

RICHARD M. DEVOS

BELIEF

In order to succeed we must first believe that we can.

MICHAEL KORDA

I found that I could find the energy . . . that I could find the determination to keep on going. I learned that your mind can amaze your body, if you just keep telling yourself, I can do it . . . I can do it . . . I can do it!

JON ERICKSON

In the moment that you carry this conviction . . . in that moment your dream will become a reality.

ROBERT COLLIER

Whether you think you can or think you can't—you are right.

HENRY FORD

You have a remarkable ability which you never acknowledged before. It is to look at a situation and know whether you can do it. And I mean really know the answer . . .

CARL FREDERICK

We can do only what we think we can do. We can be only what we think we can be. We can have only what we think we can have. What we do, what we are, what we have, all depend upon what we think.

ROBERT COLLIER

BELIEF

The first and most important step toward . . . success is the feeling that we can succeed.

NELSON BOSWELL

The strongest single factor in prosperity consciousness is self-esteem: believing you can do it, believing you deserve it, believing you will get it.

JERRY GILLIES

The mind is the limit. As long as the mind can envision the fact that you can do something, you can do it—as long as you really believe 100 percent.

ARNOLD SCHWARZENEGGER

A man is literally what he thinks.

JAMES ALLEN

The only limit to our realization of tomorrow will be our doubts of today.

FRANKLIN D. ROOSEVELT

The barrier between . . . success is not something which exists in the real world; it is composed purely and simply of . . . doubts about . . . ability.

MARK CAINE

These, then, are my last words to you: Be not afraid of life. Believe that life is worth living and your belief will help create the fact.

WILLIAM JAMES

COURAGE

Courage is a special kind of knowledge; the knowledge of how to fear what ought to be feared, and how not to fear what ought not to be feared. From this knowledge comes an inner strength that subconsciously inspires us to push on in the face of great difficulty. What can seem impossible is often possible, with courage.

You gain strength, courage and confidence by every experience which you must stop and look fear in the face...You must do the thing you think you cannot do.

ELEANOR ROOSEVELT

One man with courage is a majority.

ANDREW JACKSON

The scars you acquire by exercising courage will never make you feel inferior.

D.A. BATTISTA

COURAGE

Courage is doing what you're afraid to do. There can be no courage unless you're scared.

EDDIE RICKENBACKER

He who loses wealth loses much; he who loses a friend loses more; but he that loses courage loses all.

CERVANTES

Success is never final, and failure is never fatal; it's courage that counts.

UNKNOWN

All of the significant battles are waged within the self.

SHELDON KOPP

This is the test of your manhood: How much is there left in you after you have lost everything outside of yourself?

ORISON SWETT MARDEN

If I were asked to give what I consider the single most useful bit of advice for all humanity it would be this: Expect trouble as an inevitable part of life and when it comes, hold your head high, look it squarely in the eye and say, "I will be bigger than you. You cannot defeat me."

ANN LANDERS

Courage is resistance to fear, mastery of fear - not absence of fear.

MARK TWAIN

COURAGE

Nothing splendid has ever been achieved except by those who dared believe that something inside of them was superior to circumstance.

BRUCE BARTON

Courage is the capacity to confront what can be imagined...

LEO ROSTEN

True courage is a result of reasoning. A brave mind is always impregnable.

JEREMY COLLIER

Little minds attain and are subdued by misfortunes; but great minds rise above them.

WASHINGTON IRVING

Obstacles will look large or small to you according to whether you are large or small.

ORISON SWETT MARDEN

What the superior man seeks is in himself: what the small man seeks is in others.

FRANCOIS LA ROCHEFOUCAULD

Stone walls do not a prison make, nor iron bars a cage.

RICHARD LOVELACE

DESIRE

Desire alone is not enough. But to lack desire, means to lack a key ingredient to success. Many a talented individual failed because they lacked desire. Many victories have been snatched by the underdog because they wanted it more. So if you desire -- intensely -- and you act upon it, then everything stands within your reach.

Nothing is impossible to a willing heart.

JOHN HEYWOOD

If you only care enough for a result, you will almost certainly attain it.

WILLIAM JAMES

For the resolute and determined there is time and opportunity.

RALPH WALDO EMERSON

Through some strange and powerful principle of "mental chemistry" which she has never divulged, Nature wraps up in the impulse of strong desire, "that something" which recognizes no such word as "impossible", and accepts no such reality as failure.

NAPOLEON HILL

DESIRE

All our dreams can come true—if we have the courage to pursue them.

WALT DISNEY

The starting point of all achievement is desire. Keep this constantly in mind. Weak desires bring weak results, just as a small amount of fire makes a small amount of heat.

NAPOLEON HILL

The greatest trouble with most of us is that our demands upon ourselves are so feeble, the call upon the great within of us so weak and intermittent that it makes no impression upon the creative energies; it lacks the force that transmutes desires into realities.

ORISON SWETT MARDEN

A strong passion for any object will ensure success, for the desire of the end will point out the means.

WILLIAM HAZLITT

It sometimes seems that intense desire creates not only its own opportunities, but its own talents.

ERIC HOFFER

The intensity of your desire governs the power with which the force is directed.

JOHN MCDONALD

Nothing stops the man who desires to achieve. Every obstacle is simply a course to develop his achievement muscle. It's a strengthening of his powers of accomplishment.

ERIC BUTTERWORTH

DESIRE

A will finds a way.

ORISON SWETT MARDEN

You can have anything you want—
if you want it badly enough. You can be
anything you want to be, have anything
you desire, accomplish anything you set
out to accomplish—if you will hold
to that desire with singleness of purpose . . .

ROBERT COLLIER

Always bear in mind that your
own resolution to succeed is more important than any other one thing.

ABRAHAM LINCOLN

I gnore what a man desires and you
ignore the very source of his power . . .

WALTER LIPPMANN

Y ou learn that, whatever you are
doing in life, obstacles don't matter very
much. Pain or other circumstances can
be there, but if you want to do a job bad
enough, you'll find a way to get it done.

JACK YOUNGBLOOD

D esire creates the power.

RAYMOND HOLLIWELL

EXCELLENCE

Going far beyond the call of duty, doing more than others expect...this is what excellence is all about. And it comes from striving, maintaining the highest standards, looking after the smallest detail, and going the extra mile. Excellence means doing your very best. In everything. In everyway.

There is an infinite difference between a little wrong and just right, between fairly good and the best, between mediocrity and superiority . . .

ORISON SWETT MARDEN

Success has always been easy to measure. It is the distance between one's origins and one's final achievement . . .

MICHAEL KORDA

If a man has done his best, what else is there?

GEORGE S. PATTON

EXCELLENCE

Success is the maxium utilization of the ability that you have.

ZIG ZIGLAR

When a man has done his best, has given his all, and in the process supplied the needs of his family and his society, that man has succeeded.

MACK DOUGLAS

I do the very best I know how—the very best I can; and I mean to keep on doing so until the end.

ABRAHAM LINCOLN

To be what we are, and to become what we are capable of becoming, is the only end of life.

ROBERT LOUIS STEVENSON

All successful employers are stalking men who will do the unusual, men who think, men who attract attention by performing more than is expected of them.

CHARLES M. SCHWAB

If a man has a talent and cannot use it, he has failed. If he has a talent and uses only half of it, he has partly failed. If he has a talent and learns somehow to use the whole of it, he has gloriously succeeded, and won a satisfaction and a triumph few men ever know.

THOMAS WOLFE

When a man feels throbbing within him the power to do what he undertakes as well as it can possibly be done, this is happiness, this is success.

ORISON SWETT MARDEN

EXCELLENCE

The quality of a person's life is in direct proportion to their commitment to excellence, regardless of their chosen field of endeavor.

VINCENT T. LOMBARDI

The kind of people I look for to fill top management spots are the eager beavers, the mavericks. These are the guys who try to do more than they're expected to do—they always reach.

LEE IACOCCA

A race horse that can run a mile a few seconds faster is worth twice as much. That little extra proves to be the greatest value.

JOHN D. HESS

If there's a way to do it better . . . find it.

THOMAS A. EDISON

The greatest thing a man can do in this world is to make the most possible out of the stuff that has been given him. This is success, and there is no other.

ORISON SWETT MARDEN

He who has done his best for his own time has lived for all times.

JOHANN VON SCHILLER

Always do your best. What you plant now, you will harvest later.

OG MANDINO

FAILURE

Successful people
are not afraid to fail.
They have the ability to accept
their failures and continue on,
knowing that failure is a natural
consequence of trying. The law
of failure is one of the most
powerful of all the success laws
because you only really fail
when you quit trying.

Failure is only the opportunity to more intelligently begin again.

HENRY FORD

There can be no failure to a man who has not lost his courage, his character, his self-respect, or his self-confidence. He is still a king.

ORISON SWETT MARDEN

The greatest mistake a man can make is to be afraid of making one.

ELBERT HUBBARD

FAILURE

The credit belongs to the man who is actually in the arena; whose face is marred by dust and sweat and blood; who strives valiantly; who errs and comes short again and again; who knows the great enthusiasms, the great devotions, and spends himself in a worthy cause; who at the best knows in the end the triumph of high achievement; and who at the worst, if he fails, at least fails while daring greatly . . .

THEODORE ROOSEVELT

Remember you will not always win. Some days, the most resourceful individual will taste defeat. But there is, in this case, always tomorrow—after you have done your best to achieve success today.

MAXWELL MALTZ

The successful man will profit from his mistakes and try again in a different way.

DALE CARNEGIE

No man fails who does his best . . .

ORISON SWETT MARDEN

FAILURE

No man ever achieved worth-while success who did not, at one time or other, find himself with at least one foot hanging well over the brink of failure.

NAPOLEON HILL

The difference between greatness and mediocrity is often how an individual views a mistake . . .

NELSON BOSWELL

Failure is success if we learn from it.

MALCOLM S. FORBES

The freedom to fail is vital if you're going to succeed. Most successful men fail time and time again, and it is a measure of their strength that failure merely propels them into some new attempt at success.

MICHAEL KORDA

Don't be afraid to fail. Don't waste energy trying to cover up failure. Learn from your failures and go on to the next challenge. IT'S <u>OK</u> TO FAIL. If you're not failing, you're not growing.

H. STANLEY JUDD

In some attempts, it is glorious even to fail.

LONGINUS

GOALS

The purpose of goals is to focus our attention. The mind will not reach toward achievment until it has clear objectives. The magic begins when we set goals. It is then that the switch is turned on, the current begins to flow, and the power to accomplish becomes a reality.

There is no achievement
without goals.

ROBERT J. MCKAIN

This one step—choosing a goal and
sticking to it—changes everything.

SCOTT REED

People with goals succeed because
they know where they're going.

EARL NIGHTINGALE

If you don't know where you are
going, how can you expect to get there?

BASIL S. WALSH

GOALS

There are those who travel and those who are going somewhere. They are different and yet they are the same. The success has this over his rivals: he knows where he is going.

MARK CAINE

The indespensable first step to getting the things you want out of life is this: decide what you want.

BEN STEIN

Until input (thought) is linked to a goal (purpose) there can be no intelligent accomplishment.

PAUL G. THOMAS

If a man knows not what harbor he seeks, any wind is the right wind.

SENECA

The world has the habit of making room for the man whose words and actions show that he knows where he is going.

NAPOLEON HILL

The most important thing about goals is having one.

GEOFFRY F. ABERT

A man without a purpose is like a ship without a rudder.

THOMAS CARLYLE

HONESTY

Before us lie two paths -- honesty or dishonesty. The ignorant embark on the dishonest path; the wise on the honest. For in helping others, you help yourself; in hurting others, you hurt yourself. Those who remain honest know the truth: character overshadows money, trust rises above fame. And honesty is still the best policy.

Prefer a loss to a dishonest gain; the one brings pain at the moment, the other for all time.

CHILON

Honesty is the first chapter of the book of wisdom.

THOMAS JEFFERSON

It is better to deserve honors and not have them than to have them and not deserve them.

MARK TWAIN

Choose the way of life. Choose the way of love. Choose the way of caring . . . Choose the way of goodness. It's up to you. It's your choice.

LEO BUSCAGLIA

HONESTY

There is no right way to do something wrong.

UNKNOWN

To many a man, and sometimes to a youth, there comes the opportunity to choose between honorable competence and tainted wealth . . . The young man who starts out to be poor and honorable, holds in his hand one of the strongest elements of success.

ORISON SWETT MARDEN

They're only truly great who are truly good.

GEORGE CHAPMAN

No legacy is so rich as honesty.

WILLIAM SHAKESPEARE

The glory that goes with wealth and beauty is fleeting and fragile; virtue is a possession glorious and eternal.

SALLUST

Work joyfully and peacefully, knowing that right thoughts and right efforts will inevitably bring about right results.

JAMES ALLEN

I contend that dishonesty will create a failure force that often manifests itself in other ways—ways not apparent to the outside observer.

JOSEPH SUGARMAN

HONESTY

Understand this law and you will then know, beyond room for the slightest doubt, that you are constantly punishing yourself for every wrong you commit and rewarding yourself for every act of constructive conduct in which you indulge.

NAPOLEON HILL

Everyone will experience the consequences of his own acts. If his acts are right, he'll get good consequences; if they're not, he'll suffer for it.

HARRY BROWNE

Whatever our creed, we feel that no good deed can by any possibility go unrewarded, no evil deed unpunished.

ORISON SWETT MARDEN

You cannot do wrong without suffering wrong.

RALPH WALDO EMERSON

Each time you are honest and conduct yourself with honesty, a success force will drive you toward greater success. Each time you lie, even with a little white lie, there are strong forces pushing you toward failure.

JOSEPH SUGARMAN

Rather fail with honor than succeed by fraud.

SOPHOCLES

To measure the man measure his heart.

MALCOLM S. FORBES

IMAGINATION

Seeing all possibilities, seeing all that can be done, and how it can be done, marks the power of imagination. Your imagination stands as your own personal laboratory. Here you can rehearse the possibilities, map out plans, and visualize overcoming obstacles. Imagination turns possibilities into reality.

The source and center of all man's creative power . . . is his power of making images, or the power of imagination.

ROBERT COLLIER

You see things; and you say, "Why?" But I dream things that never were; and I say, "Why not?"

GEORGE BERNARD SHAW

We are told never to cross a bridge till we come to it, but this world is owned by men who have "crossed bridges" in their imagination far ahead of the crowd.

SPEAKERS LIBRARY

IMAGINATION

Our aspirations are our possibilities.

ROBERT BROWNING

The great successful men of the world have used their imagination . . . they think ahead and create their mental picture, and then go to work materializing that picture in all its details, filling in here, adding a little there, altering this a bit and that a bit, but steadily building —steadily building.

ROBERT COLLIER

For imagination sets the goal "picture" which our automatic mechanism works on. We act, or fail to act, not because of "will", as is so commonly believed, but because of imagination.

MAXWELL MALTZ

A man's dreams are an index to his greatness.

ZADOK RABINOWITZ

Far away there in the sunshine are my highest aspirations. I may not reach them, but I can look up and see their beauty, believe in them, and try to follow where they lead.

LOUISA MAY ALCOTT

IMAGINATION

The empires of the future are empires of the mind.

WINSTON CHURCHILL

First comes thought, then organization of that thought into ideas and plans; then transformation of those plans into reality. The beginning, as you will observe, is in your imagination.

NAPOLEON HILL

All men who have achieved great things have been dreamers.

ORISON SWETT MARDEN

The entrepreneur is essentially a visualizer and an actualizer . . . He can visualize something, and when he visualizes it he sees exactly how to make it happen.

ROBERT L. SCHWARTZ

I am thought.
I can see what the
 eyes cannot see.
I can hear what the
 ears cannot hear.
I can feel what the
 heart cannot feel.

PETER NIVIO ZARLENGA

IMAGINATION

You will become as small as your controlling desire; or as great as your dominant aspiration.

JAMES ALLEN

The only limits are, as always, those of vision.

JAMES BROUGHTON

Cherish your visions and your dreams as they are the children of your soul; the blue prints of your ultimate achievements.

NAPOLEON HILL

When you cease to dream you cease to live.

MALCOLM S. FORBES

Image creates desire. You will what you imagine.

J.G. GALLIMORE

Love

Love is the most important ingredient of success. Without it, your life echoes emptiness. With it, your life vibrates warmth and meaning. Even in hardship, love shines through. Therefore, search for love -- because if you don't have it, you're not really living -- only breathing.

We are all born for love. It is the principle of existence, and its only end.

BENJAMIN DISRAELI

Love is everything. It is the key to life, and its influences are those that move the world.

RALPH WALDO TRINE

The best portion of a good man's life —his little nameless, unremembered acts of kindness and of love.

WILLIAM WORDSWORTH

You will find as you look back upon your life that the moments when you have really lived, are the moments when you have done things in a spirit of love.

HENRY DRUMMOND

LOVE

Once you have learned to love,
You will have learned to live.

UNKNOWN

Treasure the love you receive above all. It will survive long after your gold and good health have vanished.

OG MANDINO

Where there is love there is life . . .

MOHANDAS GANDHI

Love is life . . . And if you miss love, you miss life.

LEO BUSCAGLIA

Love is the only bow on life's dark cloud. It is the Morning and Evening Star. It shines upon the cradle of the babe, and sheds its radiance upon the quiet tomb. It is the Mother of Art, inspirer of poet, patriot, and philosopher. It is the air and light of every heart, builder of every home, kindler of every fire on every hearth. It was the first dream of immorality. It fills the world with melody....Love is the magician, the enchanter, that changes worthless things to joy, and makes right royal kings of common clay.

ROBERT G. INGERSOLL

He has achieved success who has lived well, laughed often, and loved much.

LOVE

The moment you have in your heart this extra-ordinary thing called love and feel the depth, the delight, the ecstacy of it, you will discover that for you the world is transformed.

J. KRISHNAMURTI

Do all things with love.

OG MANDINO

Life without love is like a tree without blossom and fruit.

KAHLIL GIBRAN

The cure for all the ills and wrongs, the cares, the sorrows, and the crimes of humanity, all lie in the one word "love." It is the divine vitality that everywhere produces and restores life.

LYDIA MARIA CHILD

Life in abundance comes only through great love.

ELBERT HUBBARD

Love is the immortal flow of energy that nourishes, extends and preserves. Its eternal goal is life.

SMILEY BLANTON

What force is more potent than love?

IGOR STRAVINSKY

OPPORTUNITY

There are no limits to our opportunities. Most of us see only a small portion of what is possible. We create opportunities by seeing the possibilities, and having the persistence to act upon them. We must always remember... Opportunities are always here, but we must look for them.

Problems are only opportunities in work clothes.

HENRY J. KAISER

Opportunities? They are all around us . . . There is power lying latent everywhere waiting for the observant eye to discover it.

ORISON SWETT MARDEN

We don't need more strength or more ability or greater opportunity. What we need is to use what we have.

BASIL S. WALSH

OPPORTUNITY

Most successful men have not achieved their distinction by having some new talent or opportunity presented to them. They have developed the opportunity that was at hand.

BRUCE BARTON

There is no future in any job. The future lies in the man who holds the job.

GEORGE CRANE

Opportunity . . . Often it comes disguised in the form of misfortune, or temporary defeat.

NAPOLEON HILL

A wise man will make more opportunities than he finds.

FRANCIS BACON

In the middle of difficulty lies opportunity.

ALBERT EINSTEIN

Each problem has hidden in it an opportunity so powerful that it literally dwarfs the problem. The greatest success stories were created by people who recognized a problem and turned it into an opportunity.

JOSEPH SUGARMAN

OPPORTUNITY

Opportunity rarely knocks on your door. Knock rather on opportunity's door if you ardently wish to enter.

B.C. FORBES

Destiny is not a matter of chance; it is a matter of choice. It is not something to be waited for; but, rather something to be achieved.

WILLIAM JENNINGS BRYAN

The people who get on in this world are the people who get up and look for the circumstances they want, and, if they can't find them, make them.

GEORGE BERNARD SHAW

Success doesn't come to you . . .
you go to it.

MARVA COLLINS

The lure of the distant and the difficult is deceptive. The great opportunity is where you are.

JOHN BURROUGHS

Every situation, properly perceived, becomes an opportunity . . .

HELEN SCHUCMAN
AND WILLIAM THETFORD

The golden opportunity you are seeking is in yourself. It is not in your environment; it is not in luck or chance, or the help of others; it is in yourself alone.

ORISON SWETT MARDEN

PERSISTENCE

The power to hold on in spite of everything, the power to endure - this is the winner's quality. Persistence is the ability to face defeat again and again without giving up -- to push on in the face of great difficulty, knowing that victory can be yours. Persistence means taking pains to overcome every obstacle, and to do what's necessary to reach your goals.

I do not think there is any other quality so essential to success of any kind as the quality of perseverance. It overcomes almost everything, even nature.

JOHN D. ROCKEFELLER

What this power is I cannot say; all I know is that it exists and it becomes available only when a man is in that state of mind in which he knows exactly what he wants and is fully determined not to quit until he finds it.

ALEXANDER GRAHAM BELL

Our greatest glory is not in never falling, but in rising every time we fall.

CONFUCIUS

PERSISTENCE

History has demonstrated that the most notable winners usually encountered heartbreaking obstacles before they triumphed. They won because they refused to become discouraged by their defeats.

B.C. FORBES

Success . . . seems to be connected with action. Successful men keep moving. They make mistakes, but they don't quit.

CONRAD HILTON

Success seems to be largely a matter of hanging on after others have let go.

WILLIAM FEATHER

Effort only fully releases its reward after a person refuses to quit.

NAPOLEON HILL

Most people give up just when they're about to achieve success. They quit on the one yard line. They give up at the last minute of the game one foot from a winning touchdown.

H. ROSS PEROT

All great achievements require time.

DAVID JOSEPH SCHWARTZ

PERSISTENCE

It's the constant and determined effort that breaks down all resistance, sweeps away all obstacles.

CLAUDE M. BRISTOL

The majority of men meet with failure because of their lack of persistence in creating new plans to take the place of those which fail.

NAPOLEON HILL

Few things are impossible to diligence and skill . . . Great works are performed not by strength, but perseverance.

SAMUEL JOHNSON

Success is failure turned inside out,
The silver tint of the clouds of doubt,
And you never can tell how close
   you are,
It may be near when it seems so far.
So stick to the fight when you're
   hardest hit,
It's when things seem worse,
That you must not quit.

UNKNOWN

He conquers who endures.

PERSIUS

PERSISTENCE

The rewards for those who persevere far exceed the pain that must precede the victory.

**TED ENGSTROM
AND R. ALEC MACKENZIE**

If you can force your heart and nerve and sinew to serve your turn long after they are gone, And so hold on when there is nothing in you Except the Will which says to them: "Hold on!"

RUDYARD KIPLING

To endure is greater than to dare; to tire out hostile fortune; to be daunted by no difficulty; to keep heart when all have lost it—who can say this is not greatness?

WILLIAM MAKEPEACE THACKERAY

Nothing in the world can take the place of persistence. Talent will not; nothing is more common than unsuccessful men with talent. Genius will not; unrewarded genius is almost a proverb. Education will not; the world is full of educated derelicts. Persistence and determination alone are omnipotent.

CALVIN COOLIDGE

RESPONSIBILITY

The fulfillment of your dreams lies within you and you alone. When you understand and accept this, then nothing, or no one, can deny you greatness. The power to succeed or fail is yours. And no one can take that away.

The day you take complete responsibility for yourself, the day you stop making any excuses, that's the day you start to the top.

O.J. SIMPSON

More powerful than all the success slogans ever penned by human hand is the realization for every man that he has but one boss. That boss is the man—he—himself.

GABRIEL HEATTER

Some men have thousands of reasons why they cannot do what they want to, when all they need is one reason why they can.

WILLIS R. WHITNEY

RESPONSIBILITY

Success on any major scale requires you to accept responsibility . . . In the final analysis, the one quality that all successful people have . . . is the ability to take on responsibility.

MICHAEL KORDA

I was taught very early that I would have to depend entirely upon myself; that my future lay in my own hands.

DARIUS OGDEN MILLS

There is a kind of elevation which does not depend on fortune; it is a certain air which distinguishes us, and seems to destine us for great things; it is a price which we imperceptibly set upon ourselves.

FRANCOIS DE LA ROCHEFOUCAULD

The mould of a man's fortune is in his own hands.

FRANCIS BACON

Hold yourself responsible for a higher standard than anybody else expects of you. Never excuse yourself.

HENRY WARD BEECHER

Nothing happens by itself . . . It all will come your way, once you understand that you have to make it come your way, by your own exertions.

BEN STEIN

Life will always be to a large extent what we ourselves make it.

SAMUEL SMILES

RESPONSIBILITY

We have forty million reasons for failure, but not a single excuse.

RUDYARD KIPLING

As human beings, we are endowed with freedom of choice, and we cannot shuffle off our responsibility upon the shoulders of God or nature. We must shoulder it ourselves. It is up to us.

ARNOLD J. TOYNBEE

A man carries his success or his failure with him . . . it does not depend on outside conditions . . .

RALPH WALDO TRINE

Not in time, place, or circumstances, but in the man lies success . . .

CHARLES B. ROUSS

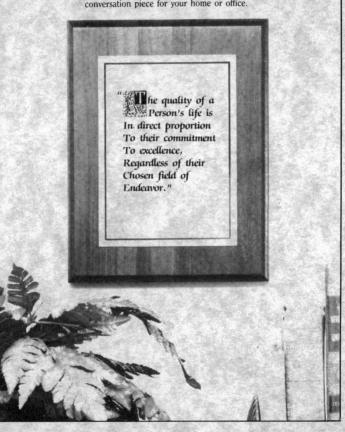

Order Your Favorite Quote Today!

Timeless... Your favorite quote on a beautiful brass plate mounted on a walnut finished base. A real conversation piece for your home or office.

"The quality of a
Person's life is
In direct proportion
To their commitment
To excellence,
Regardless of their
Chosen field of
Endeavor."

PRICE LIST

	BRASS PLAQUE
	Beautiful brass plate mounted on walnut finished base. Outside dimensions - 8 x 10.
1	$25.00
2-10	$19.00
11-25	$17.00

Over 25: please call for custom quote.

Shipping and handling:
Add $3.00 per unit on quantities of 1-10.
Add $2.50 per unit on quantities of 11-25.

MAIL ORDER FORM TO:

GREAT QUOTATIONS, INC.
919 SPRINGER DRIVE • LOMBARD, IL 60148

TOLL FREE: 800-621-1432 (outside of Illinois)
(312) 953-1222

Other Great Quotations Books:

- Best of Success
- Business Quotes
- Commitment to Excellence
- Golf Quotes
- Great Quotes / Great Women
- Humorous Quotes
- Inspirational Quotes
- Loving You Is Easy
- Motivational Quotes
- Over The Hill
- Sports Quotes

ORDER FORM

QTY	PRODUCT	QUOTE PAGE NUMBER	UNIT PRICE	TOTAL PRICE
				.

MAIL ORDER FORM TO:

GREAT QUOTATIONS, INC.
919 Springer Drive
Lombard, Illinois 60148-6416
Local (312) 953-1222
Toll-Free 800-621-1432

SUBTOTAL	$
6 ¼ % SALES TAX (IL RES.)	$
SHIPPING & HANDLING	$
TOTAL	$

NAME _____

ADDRESS _____

CITY_____ STATE_____ ZIP_____

Phone Number ( ) _____

Enclosed is my check or money order for $ made out to Great Quotations, Inc.

Charge my ☐ VISA   ☐ MASTER CARD

Card Number_____ Exp. date_____

Signature _____